THE BATTLE OF
WATERLOO

Russell Roberts

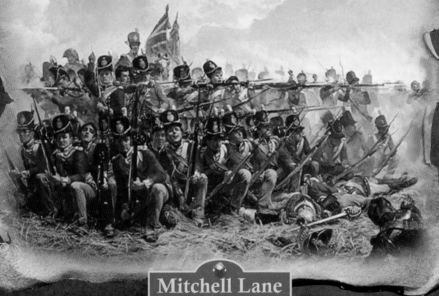

Mitchell Lane
PUBLISHERS

P.O. Box 196
Hockessin, Delaware 19707
Visit us on the web: www.mitchelllane.com
Comments? email us: mitchelllane@mitchelllane.com

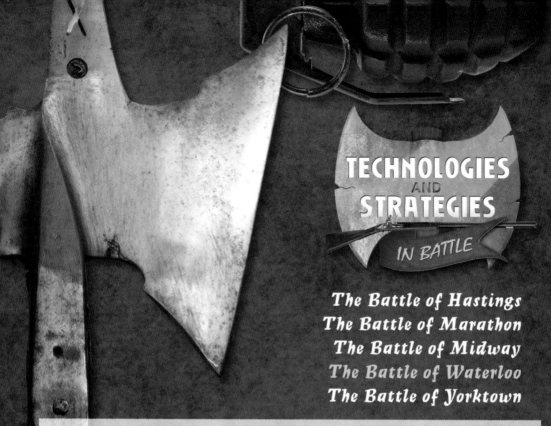

TECHNOLOGIES AND STRATEGIES
IN BATTLE

The Battle of Hastings
The Battle of Marathon
The Battle of Midway
The Battle of Waterloo
The Battle of Yorktown

ABOUT THE AUTHOR: Russell Roberts has written
and published nearly 40 books for adults and
children on a variety of subjects, including
baseball, memory power, business, New Jersey
history, and travel. He has written numerous
books for Mitchell Lane Publishers, including
*Nathaniel Hawthorne, Holidays and
Celebrations in Colonial America, What's So
Great About Daniel Boone, The Life and Times
of Nostradamus, Poseidon,* and *The Cyclopes.*
He lives in Bordentown, New Jersey, with his
family and a fat, fuzzy, and crafty calico cat
named Rusti.

PUBLISHER'S NOTE: The facts on which this book
is based have been thoroughly researched.
Documentation of such research can be
found on page 46. While every possible effort
has been made to ensure accuracy, the
publisher will not assume liability for damages
caused by inaccuracies in the data, and
makes no warranty on the accuracy of the
information contained herein.

Printing   1   2   3   4   5   6   7   8   9

**Library of Congress
Cataloging-in-Publication Data**

Roberts, Russell, 1953–
 The Battle of Waterloo / by Russell Roberts.
    p. cm. — (Technologies and strategies in
battle)
 Includes bibliographical references and index.
 ISBN 978-1-61228-076-9 (library bound)
 1. Waterloo, Battle of, Waterloo, Belgium,
1815—Juvenile literature. 2. Napoleon I,
Emperor of the French, 1769-1821—Military
leadership—Juvenile literature. 3. Napoleonic
Wars, 1800-1815—Campaigns—Belgium—
Waterloo—Juvenile literature. I. Title.
 DC242.R735 2011
 940.2'742—dc22

                                        2011006174

eBook ISBN: 9781612281582

                                              PLB

CONTENTS

Chapter 1

With a splintering crash, the locked gate of the Hougoumont farm courtyard burst open. Sous-Lieutenant Legros, a huge French soldier nicknamed *l'Enforceur* who had smashed the wooden gate open, burst inside the courtyard with a triumphant cry, brandishing a giant ax. Thirty more French soldiers followed him inside, all firing their muskets and shouting.

With a great cry of their own, a band of British soldiers rushed to meet the French and stop them from getting any farther into the courtyard. Both sides shot at the other, the British from their positions inside the courtyard and the French from just inside the gate as they tried to force themselves into the area. The courtyard quickly filled with dense clouds of gunpowder smoke, making it nearly impossible to determine friend from foe. Choking, coughing, gasping for breath, stumbling over the bodies of the dead, the two groups of soldiers shot, stabbed, and clubbed each other in the smoky dimness. The cries of the dying filled the air as both the English and French struggled for possession of Hougoumont.

It was a critical moment early in the Battle of Waterloo.

The Fight for Hougoumont

On June 18, 1815, an army of 77,000 French soldiers commanded by Napoléon Bonaparte had attacked a British force of 73,000 led by Arthur Wellesley, the Duke of Wellington. (Wellington's army was actually composed of German and Dutch soldiers, as well as other nationalities, including British. For convenience here they will be referred to as the British Army.) The battle was near a tiny village in modern-day Belgium called Waterloo.

For Napoléon Bonaparte, even to be at Waterloo was surprising. Six months before, he had been living in exile on a tiny island off the coast of Italy called Elba. That had been quite a downfall for someone who was once the most powerful man in the world and had kings and the Pope ready to do his bidding.

However, in 1814, a coalition of various European countries

defeated Napoléon, forcing him to abdicate his position as the emperor of France. The victorious allies sent him to Elba and thought they'd seen the last of him.

They were wrong. Less than one year later Napoléon returned to France, rebuilt his army, and again was a threat to the peace and safety of Europe. Quickly Britain, Prussia, Russia, Austria, and the Netherlands determined to raise soldiers for a new army and meet Napoléon in battle once again.

Napoléon's strategy against all these enemies was simple: attack them individually before they could combine into an overwhelming force and crush him.[1] His first targets were the British Army of Wellington and the Prussian Army of Gebhard von Blücher, which were trying to come together close to the northeastern French border. Napoléon decided to attack them separately, before they could combine forces.

By so doing, Napoléon was following one of his cardinal strategies of warfare: Always go on the offensive. Even when his enemies might have superior numbers, Napoléon tried to make them respond to him and what he was doing. He had used this strategy successfully for many years.

Moving quicker than the British or Prussians thought possible, Napoléon left Paris on the evening of June 11 with his army and was in Belgium on June 15.[2] He fought and defeated the Prussians at Ligny on June 16. Now, on June 18, it was time for him to face Wellington.

Capturing the Hougoumont farmhouse complex was critical to Napoléon's chances for success at Waterloo. The farmhouse itself was attached to other buildings, including a barn, two smaller houses, and a chapel. There were also a formal garden and an orchard. Walls enclosed the complex. A small wooded area stood between the side of Hougoumont and the French.

Hougoumont was a key position in the British defensive strategy. The French could not just go around it or ignore it as they launched their attacks; the British troops inside the farmhouse could blast to smithereens any French soldiers who came near it, which would disrupt any attack plan. No wonder that Wellington told the Hougoumont commander, Lieutenant

Legros l'Enforceur uses an ax to burst through the gates of Hougoumont and charge the British defenders.

Colonel James Macdonnell, that the position had to be held at all costs.[3]

Around 11:30 A.M., French troops commanded by Napoléon's youngest brother, Prince Jérôme, launched an assault on the nearly 2,600 British soldiers who occupied Hougoumont and the surrounding area. The fighting was savage. Muskets cracked and blazed. Men screamed in pain. Bayonets and knives sliced through the air as the soldiers lunged and stabbed one another.

At one point the British troops in the woods retreated into Hougoumont's courtyard and orchard. The French soldiers surged forward. But the retreat had been prearranged, done to lure the

French into British territory. Gunfire erupted from the buildings and the walls of Hougoumont. The British fired from behind trees in the orchard, from holes cut in the walls of the complex, and from rooftops. The mass of French soldiers reeled back in distress under the hail of bullets. French casualties lay strewn on the ground.

But the remaining French troops recovered, regrouped, and stormed Hougoumont again. Some of them rushed up and tried to grab the short, exposed portion of the British musket barrels that were protruding from the walls and wrestle them away.[4]

The Hougoumont farm was well fortified, with walls of stone and brick.

The British responded by firing directly at the Frenchmen, or, in many cases, jabbing at them with their bayonets.

Finally the French fell back. Dead and dying men, contorted in agony, lay scattered on the blood-soaked ground. The British relaxed—but not for long. Jérôme Bonaparte's units, reinforced now, again surged toward Hougoumont. They retook the areas from which they had just retreated and pressed in close to the defenders. Wellington sent reinforcements to help his beleaguered troops.

When Sous-Lieutenant Legros shattered the lock and burst into the courtyard with thirty men, the British defenders rushed to meet them. Would the French be able to pour more soldiers into the courtyard and overrun the British defenders? Would the British be able to stop them?

Muskets

The primary weapon used by the infantry soldiers of both sides at Waterloo was the musket. Muskets had been used in various parts of Europe and Asia for many years before Waterloo. They required a cumbersome, multistep process to load and fire them, so only about three or four shots could be fired within one minute's time. Retreating soldiers or those dealing with the stress of battle were even slower to fire. (The sight of a mass of enemy soldiers advancing right at him was enough to stress out any soldier.)

Even when soldiers were in perfect formation, they would sometimes forget to actually fire their muskets after they loaded them. There are many reports of muskets found after a battle that had been repeatedly loaded but never fired.

Muskets were not accurate, and they tended to misfire or jam. At most a musket was accurate within 100 paces of the target. If the soldier's cartridge got wet or if there was a great deal of humidity in the air, his musket would not fire.

To compensate for these drawbacks, infantrymen were grouped close together when they attacked. The idea was that many muskets firing at once had a better chance of inflicting damage on the enemy. Unfortunately, the close formation also made the soldiers easy targets for the enemy. Musket fire also produced clouds of smoke so thick that once a battle started, soldiers could not see where the enemy was.

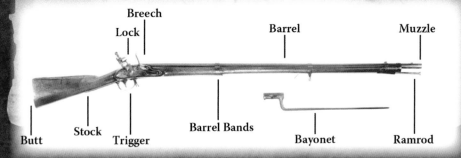

Breech

Lock

Barrel

Muzzle

Butt

Stock

Trigger

Barrel Bands

Bayonet

Ramrod

Napoléon Bonaparte was born on August 15, 1769, in Ajaccio, a town on the island of Corsica. For centuries Corsica, which is located west of modern-day Italy in the Mediterranean Sea, was ruled by Genoa (a country that later became part of Italy). In 1764, France purchased Corsica from Genoa. The Corsican people revolted, but the French defeated them decisively in May 1769. Two of the Corsican freedom fighters were Carlo Buonaparte and his young wife, Letizia. On August 15, she gave birth to a baby boy, named Napoleone after a recently deceased uncle.

Napoléon was born with a caul—part of the birth membrane that covers the head—which in many societies, including Corsican, was considered lucky.[1] When he was ten he went to military school in the town of Brienne, France. In October 1784 he was selected for the prestigious École military academy in Paris. At barely sixteen years old, Napoléon was commissioned a second lieutenant in the French military and was sent to join a regiment in Valence, near Corsica and his family.

At Valence Napoléon first wore the uniform that he would

Captain Cannon

forever consider the nicest in the world—a French artillery uniform. It consisted of a blue coat with scarlet outlining the pockets, a blue waistcoat and pants, yellow buttons, gold-fringed epaulettes (a shoulder decoration on a uniform that signifies rank), and a black hat.[2]

As an artilleryman, Napoléon became an expert at handling and using the smoothbore muzzle-loading cannon of the time. Like the smoothbore musket, these cannons were not as accurate as the rifled ordnance that came later. To fire one of these cannons, a soldier ignited a cord at the back of the weapon. After it fired, it recoiled (jerked backward) five or six feet, and then had to be moved—wrestled is more like it—back into place before being fired again.

The ammunition these cannons fired were of several types: solid shot (a cannon

ball), explosive shell, canister (a metal canister filled with small metal balls that, when fired, disintegrated and sent the balls on their way), grapeshot (similar to canister, but filled with metal balls, glass, rocks, metal links, or other types of shrapnel), and hot shot (projectiles that were heated to a high temperature before they were fired).

These cannons were named for the weight of the object they fired. Twelve-pounders and heavier guns could usually fire one round per minute, while lighter guns could fire two.

During the Battle of Toulon in 1793, Napoléon demonstrated great skill with cannons, and he received a lot of attention for his accomplishments. For this, a jealous superior officer nicknamed Napoléon "Captain Cannon."

On October 5, 1795, when he used cannons to turn back protesters who were trying to bring down the French government in Paris, Napoléon rose to national prominence. "God fights on the side of the best artillery,"[3] he said, and he proved it with an astonishing series of military victories. Because of these successes, on December 2, 1804, he was crowned emperor of France.

More cannon! More cannon! That was Napoléon's constant cry in every battle before and after he became emperor. During

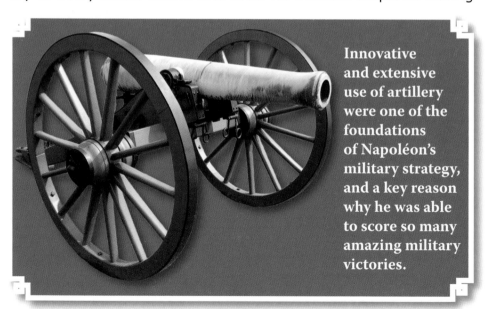

Innovative and extensive use of artillery were one of the foundations of Napoléon's military strategy, and a key reason why he was able to score so many amazing military victories.

Round shots

Grape shot

Cannons could fire many types of projectiles, though the spherical balls were more accurate than the others.

the French Revolution, artillery designers and manufacturers had reduced the weight and length of the cannon barrel. They had also reduced the weight and improved the wheels of the gun carriage. These cannons were much more mobile. A team of six or eight large horses could haul a twelve-pounder cannon fairly easily, while it took just four to six horses to pull one of the lighter guns.[4] At the same time, cannon balls and other projectiles were manufactured with more precision, so they could be fired with more accuracy.

Napoléon used these new artillery guns with great effect to win victory after victory on the battlefield. "It is with artillery that war is made," he said.[5] He moved his artillery wherever he needed it, frequently grouping guns together to blast the enemy with a massive barrage.

Nowhere was this perhaps better proved than against the Russians on June 14, 1807, at the Battle of Friedland. His guns, placed 600 paces from the Russians, were the first to be fired. Napoléon kept moving the guns forward until they were merely

60 paces from the enemy—practically point-blank range. Finally the Russians retreated, leaving behind 25,000 casualties. The French lost only a third as many.

Napoléon knew that artillery, effectively used, could usually prevail against infantry. "Good infantry is without doubt the backbone of the army; but if it has to fight a long time against very superior artillery, it will become demoralized and will be destroyed," he said.[6]

Thanks in large part to his expert use of artillery,[7] by the beginning of 1808 Napoléon ruled half of Europe—an empire of

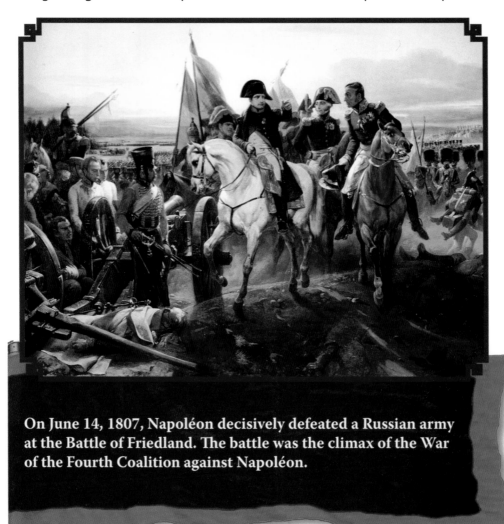

On June 14, 1807, Napoléon decisively defeated a Russian army at the Battle of Friedland. The battle was the climax of the War of the Fourth Coalition against Napoléon.

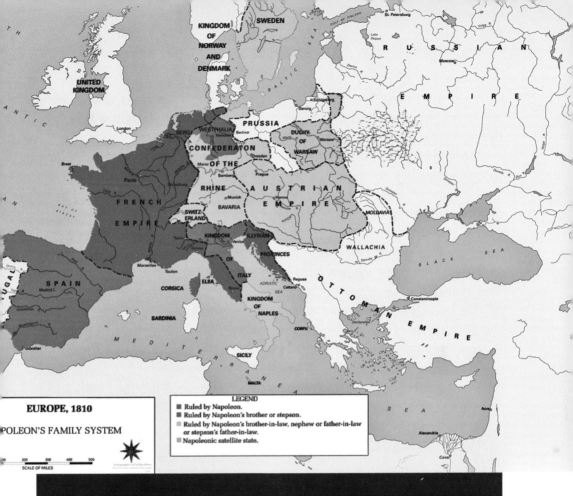

EUROPE, 1810

POLEON'S FAMILY SYSTEM

SCALE OF MILES

By 1810, Napoléon's influence spread across most of Europe.

70 million people.[8] Other countries were slow to adapt to his military tactics.

Keenly aware of the artillery's value, Napoléon ramped up France's production of cannon, from 900 to 13,000 iron cannons per year. Seventeen new iron foundries were established to assist in their manufacture.[9]

England was Napoléon's relentless enemy during this time. The British were wary of Napoléon, and did not want to come under his rule. They continually gathered other nations into groups called coalitions to wage war against France and Napoléon.

In June 1812, Napoléon invaded Russia. It was the biggest mistake of his life. Because of the vastness of Russia, the cold weather, and relentless attacks by its partisans, the French invasion failed. Napoléon's retreat from Russia is one of the most

famous events in world history. The emperor limped home with his army in shambles. Formerly the dominant military force in Europe, the French army was reduced to a shadow of itself.

Napoléon's Russian misadventure encouraged other nations to once again join together against him. After numerous battles, the forces of the Sixth Coalition captured Paris in March 1814, forcing Napoléon to abdicate one month later.

By the Treaty of Fontainebleau, Napoléon was exiled to Elba. Less than a year later he was back. He took over the French government once again and began a period that is known as The Hundred Days. The Congress of Vienna, attended by many of the countries that had defeated him initially, was interrupted by the news that Napoléon had escaped. Alarmed, England, Russia, Austria, Prussia, and the Netherlands joined together in yet another coalition—the Seventh—and vowed to defeat him once and for all. Always taking the offensive, Napoléon decided to strike first, before the armies of the coalition could come together.

Waterloo was the result of that decision.

Swedish riding artillery, used against Napoléon, 1813–1814

Napoléon's War Strategies

Napoléon found success with numerous war strategies. He never wrote them down, but people who studied his military campaigns were able to define these patterns:

1. **Objective.** Napoléon's objective was to attack the main body of his enemy's forces. Another general might have a different objective—such as destroying enemy communications—but Napoléon focused on how he could quickly put the main body of his enemy out of commission.

2. **Simple Plans.** Napoléon knew that battles are chaotic, and that complicated plans can easily get confused. He kept his plans simple and straightforward.

3. **Coordination.** Napoléon tried to have all the units of his army—infantry, cavalry, and artillery—act as one, rather than as individual pieces.

4. **Offense.** Napoléon tried to go on the offensive, rather than wait and defend his position.

5. **Maneuver.** One of Napoléon's great strengths as a military commander was his ability to maneuver his army. Even when the enemy outnumbered him, he was usually able to get more of his men to the critical points in the battle. He left fewer soldiers than normal in non-crucial areas, such as guarding supplies.

6. **Surprise.** Napoléon moved his troops quickly and attacked in unexpected places—all to gain the element of surprise.

7. **Security.** Knowing how effective surprise was, Napoléon tried to avoid being surprised himself by keeping his forces as safe and secure as possible from enemy attack.

Wellington called his victory at Waterloo "the nearest run-thing you ever saw in your life," meaning that the battle was very close and could have gone either way.[1] What determined its outcome, and what directly influenced the battle, were previous events.

When Napoléon initially returned to France from Elba on March 1, 1815, he had hoped to regain the French throne from King Louis XVIII without fighting. The king did indeed flee Paris before him, leaving Napoléon in charge. But the nations of Europe at the Congress of Vienna declared Napoléon an enemy to world peace and pledged to defeat him. With war inevitable, Napoléon knew that his only chance was to attack the armies of the Seventh Coalition individually, before they could unite as one unstoppable force. He decided to march into what is now Belgium and attack the British troops of Wellington and the Prussian troops under Field Marshal Blücher.

There was another advantage to attacking first. Many of the top British troops had been sent to the United States to serve in the War of 1812. The remaining troops in Wellington's army had

Why Waterloo?

not yet fought Napoléon, and therefore, Napoléon reasoned, they might be easier to defeat. Wellington admitted as such, calling his army "very weak and ill-equipped."[2]

Napoléon also likely had his doubts about the Prussian troops under Blücher. Although the Prussian soldiers were good fighters and Blücher had a reputation as a tough general, he also suffered from hallucinations, and he may have been mentally ill. He believed, for example, that the French had made the floor of his rooms so hot that it burned his feet.[3]

Napoléon also knew that his own army was far from the superior fighting force of the past. Years of almost continual fighting and the resulting casualties had diluted the quality of his troops. Napoléon would have to rely more than ever on a favored strategy: the mass artillery bombardment. He

needed to let the artillery soften up the enemy as much as possible before he attacked in closer combat.

On Thursday, June 15, 1815, Napoléon and his troops crossed into what is now Belgium. He attacked and overran the village of Charleroi, which had been held by the Prussians. This gave the French a clear road to the large city of Brussels.

Meanwhile, Wellington had spent the night before at a ball given by the Duchess of Richmond in Brussels. The ball had been planned for weeks, during a time when Wellington did not think that major military operations against Napoléon would get under way until July. However, Napoléon had moved quickly, and this surprised Wellington. "Napoléon has humbugged me, by God!" he said upon learning of Napoléon's whereabouts. "He has gained twenty-four hours march on me."[4]

Many have criticized Wellington for attending a party on the night that Napoléon had already brushed aside the Prussians and was rushing toward him. However, Wellington had not been certain of Napoléon's movements until just before the ball. As soon as he found out, he ordered his army to concentrate at Quatre Bras. Thus he had already done everything he could do by the night of the ball. By attending the ball, Wellington was showing the people of Brussels that there was no need to panic. In addition, the ball was well attended by Wellington's officers. This allowed him to quickly issue orders to his men, and this is precisely what he did. Some of his officers did not even have time to change their clothes, and went off to fight in their fancy evening attire.[5]

Meanwhile, Napoléon had split his troops. Some he sent to Quatre Bras under the command of Marshal Michel Ney, with orders to take the village. He took the remaining French troops east to the village of Ligny to attack the Prussian army that was there. (Most of these "villages" were not towns in the usual sense, but just a few huts grouped together.)

On June 16, 1815, two battles occurred only seven miles apart. The first was between the French and the British at Quatre Bras. Ney did not attack aggressively at the beginning, and by

One of Wellington's favorite clothing items was a stylish modification of the Hessian boot. The boot was almost knee high, and was very close fitting, making them suitable for the muddy battlefield. Because of Wellington's popularity, this boot style became known as the Wellington. Later made of rubber, Wellies were used extensively during World War II and by civilians around the world.

the time he did so Wellington was on the scene. This battle was a draw.

The second battle was between Napoléon and Blücher at Ligny, and resulted in a defeat for the Prussians. They lost 16,000 soldiers killed or wounded and were forced to retreat.

The Prussian Army marched north to the village of Wavre. If they had gone east into Prussia, as might be expected, the Prussians would have not been able to connect with Wellington's forces and would have essentially taken themselves out of the war. However, by moving north, the Prussians assured that they would be able to join up with Wellington. Despite their loss at Ligny, they were still a force to be reckoned with.

The Prussian defeat at Ligny forced Wellington to abandon his position at Quatre Bras. Napoléon trumpeted this outcome as a total victory over both the British and the Prussian armies. Paris celebrated the news.

With Napoléon in a position to sweep the retreating armies from the field, on the morning of the next day, June 17, he did . . . nothing. This was completely out of character for him. Throughout his military career, Napoléon had been successful because he had always acted swiftly and ruthlessly, especially when the enemy was retreating.

Chapter 3

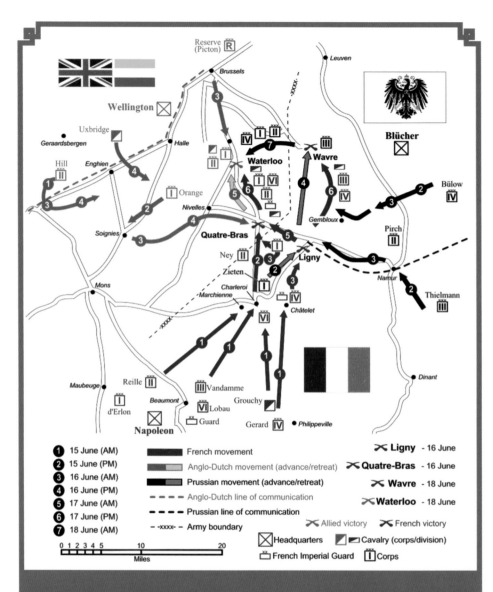

The Battle of Waterloo was the climax of several battles before it. Napoléon hoped to drive a wedge between the Prussian army and the English before they could join forces and overwhelm him. He thought he had defeated the Prussians at Ligny, but he was wrong, and it cost him dearly at Waterloo.

Historians have long debated why Napoléon did not pounce on either the retreating British or Prussians on the morning of June 17. No one knows why he spent the time dictating letters, examining the Ligny battlefield, and talking to his troops, but that's exactly what he did. Then he did something even more out of character: he detached one of his commanders, Marshal Emmanuel de Grouchy, and 30,000 troops to follow and harass the Prussians at Wavre. Napoléon had maintained that a general should never divide his forces before a major battle. Yet that is precisely what he did. The absence of these 30,000 troops during the Battle of Waterloo would prove critical.

Even more important, if Grouchy had pursued the Prussians aggressively, he might have been able to stop them from coming to Wellington's aid. But Grouchy did not. By the end of the day he had moved just seven miles—a snail's pace.

Another factor in the Battle of Waterloo was the weather. The rain poured down, making it difficult for men, horses, or artillery to move very fast on dirt roads that quickly turned to mud. As British soldier William Wheeler remembered: "The water ran in

While the rain poured down on the troops at Ligny, Napoléon dictated letters from his quarters. For officers, tents could be erected and disassembled quickly. On the British side, the bell tent was merely spread out and staked, then the center pole erected. At 12 feet (4 meters) in diameter, it was quite roomy.

Gebhard von Blücher was instrumental in the 1814 defeat of Napoléon. At age 72, Blücher came out of retirement to face him again.

streams from the cuffs of our jackets . . . we were wet as if we were plunged overhead in a river." Another soldier wrote that it was as if the water were being poured out of the sky from overturned tubs.[6]

By the morning of Sunday, June 18, Wellington had his men situated at the foot of a small hill called Mont St. Jean, south of the village of Waterloo. It was a strong defensive position that Wellington had already personally scouted; it blocked the road to Brussels for Napoléon. Wellington had Blücher's promise that the Prussians, far from being a defeated force as Napoléon thought, were going to come to his aid from Wavre, about ten miles away. Knowing that the Prussians were going to assist him, Wellington decided to make a stand at Mont St. Jean. The battle would become known as Waterloo.

Wellington placed his troops and waited for Napoléon. The night before, when one of his officers asked him what his plans were, Wellington indicated that everything depended upon Napoléon—he would only react to Napoléon's actions. Then he said: "There is one thing certain . . . that whatever happens, you and I will do our duty."[7]

The stage was set for one of the most famous battles of all time.

The Duke of Wellington

Arthur Wesley was born in Dublin, Ireland, on May 1, 1769. In 1798 his family changed its last name to Wellesley. However, Arthur will always be known by his title: The Duke of Wellington.

Early in life there was no indication that Wellington would one day become famous. His three years as a student at the famous English school Eton (1781–1784) were uninspiring.

Without a concrete career path, and with a dwindling family fortune, Wellington joined the military in March 1787. There he seemed to find himself. After he was rejected as a suitable candidate for marriage because he had no prospects, he determined to concentrate on his military career. With borrowed money he purchased higher and higher ranks in the British Army (a common practice at this time).

In 1796 he went to India and achieved numerous military successes, including a victory at the Battle of Assaye (1803). When he returned to England he was knighted and became a member of parliament. However, the army was in his blood, and he left politics in 1807 to join a military expedition to Denmark.

By this time Napoléon was a threat. In 1808 Wellington was put in command of the allied forces against Napoléon in the Peninsular War, which lasted from 1808 to 1814 and eventually forced France to withdraw from Spain and Portugal. When Napoléon subsequently abdicated, Wellington became a national hero. When Napoléon returned in 1815, Wellington was the logical choice to go against him. Wellington's victory at Waterloo finished Napoléon for good and assured Wellington's place in history.

Wellington later served as Britain's prime minister. He died on September 14, 1852.

Chapter 4

When the sun rose on the morning of June 18, Napoléon saw Wellington's troops waiting for him at Mont St. Jean. He had been afraid that the British had slipped away and escaped through the Forest of Soignes, which was directly behind their position. But they had not, and it was clear that a major battle was brewing. Pleased at the prospect, Napoléon brimmed with confidence. "Ah! Now I've got them, those English!" he said.[1]

To his generals he was even more confident. "We have ninety chances in our favour, and not ten against us," he told them.[2] Perhaps if he had known that Wellington had received a message from Blücher that morning, the French leader would not have been so sanguine. The message conveyed that virtually the entire Prussian Army was en route from Wavre—Blücher had left just a small force at Wavre to deal with Grouchy—and would strike Napoléon's right flank later in the day. Napoléon would have been even less confident had he realized the strength of Wellington's position. He was anchored by the Hougoumont farmhouse complex on the right and the hamlet of Papelotte on

The Battle Begins

the left. Both places were filled with British soldiers. The French could not attack either Wellington's left or right flank without getting hit by withering enemy fire from these two areas.

In the center and a bit to the left of Wellington's position was La Haye (or Haie) Sainte. Like Hougoumont, although smaller, this stout farmhouse complex contained stables, a barn, and a piggery. Once again, no French troops could pass it without receiving unbearable fire.

Finally, the terrain itself helped Wellington. Thick vegetation, sunken lanes, slopes, a cornfield, and other natural obstacles were part of the battlefield. Wellington had no intention of attacking Napoléon and was waiting for the French to come to him. The French would have to deal with all the landscape features as they made their approach.

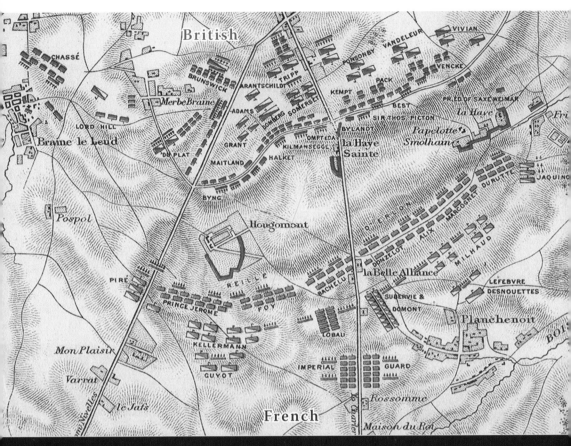

Napoléon's battle plan at Waterloo called for a frontal assault. The morning of the battle he was quite confident of victory, which is perhaps one reason that his strategy was not more elaborate.

Wellington had placed troops on the reverse slope of Mont St. Jean. Concealing soldiers in this way was a favorite strategy of his, because it hid the true strength of his forces. Since he had fought Napoléon before, he knew that the French commander liked to start battles with a massive artillery barrage. The soldiers on the reverse slope of the hill would be protected from Napoléon's gunners.

Over Napoléon's 6:00 A.M. breakfast, Jérôme reported that one of Wellington's aides had said the Prussians would arrive on the battlefield later that day. Napoléon scoffed at the report. He

believed the Prussians were defeated, and thought Grouchy could deal with them. He was relieved to see the rain had stopped, because it meant the ground would start to dry and enable him to move his artillery easier. He wanted to begin his attack at nine but delayed it, in part because of the wet ground and in part because his troops simply were not in position.

Napoléon planned a basic attack formation: a frontal assault. He wanted to split Wellington's army in two, and then deal with each piece. This would clear the road to Brussels. The French soldiers were encouraged by the idea that they could shortly be looting the rich houses of that town.[3]

The Battle of Waterloo is typically divided into five phases. The first phase began around 11:30 A.M. with a French artillery barrage. Napoléon then launched an attack against Hougoumont, but this was intended only as a diversion. He wanted Wellington to respond to this threat by committing more and more troops to Hougoumont, which would have left him with fewer men elsewhere. However, the opposite occurred. Throughout the battle, the French, not the British, poured more and more soldiers into the Hougoumont fight. Napoléon's men were not available to him at a critical moment.

The fight for Hougoumont continued all day, but the French never dislodged the British. The nearest they came was when the thirty troops led by *L'Enforceur* stormed through the gate. When several British troops raced forward and slammed the

Napoléon and his cavalry officers adopted the scimitar sword from the fierce Mameluke warriors they had defeated in Egypt in 1798. He also convinced some of these warriors to fight in his Imperial Guard. After Waterloo, troops from Britain and other countries began using the 33 ½-inch sword.

Artillery took the combined efforts of men and horses to place it in position, or to hurry and move it if need be (if it was threatened by the enemy, for example). Combine this with the fact that artillery sometimes exploded or misfired, and it's clear that an artilleryman's job was a hard one indeed!

gate closed, the thirty French were trapped inside, and others couldn't come in. The French were sitting ducks; the British defenders fired into them without mercy. When the smoke had cleared all the French were dead, except for a fourteen-year-old drummer boy. Wellington later praised the defenders, saying, "the success of the battle turned upon closing the gates of Hougoumont."[4]

Around 1:30 P.M. the second phase of the battle began. A large infantry of about 16,000 French troops under Jean-Baptiste Drouet, Count d'Erlon, assaulted the center of Wellington's army. Napoléon hoped that this would rout the British forces. However, because Wellington had placed his men on the reverse slope of the hill, his earlier artillery barrage was not as effective as Napoléon had planned.

In France, production of cannons increased to supply Napoléon's wars. This bronze six-pounder was manufactured in Douai, France, in 1813. It was captured at Waterloo and taken back to England.

As they marched forward, the French troops had to contend with muddy ground and cornfields with stalks that were six feet high. The mud canceled out Napoléon's artillery advantage. As battle historian Jeremy Black noted: "Instead of bouncing forward with deadly effect, cannonballs rested where they hit the ground."[5]

The two sides battled desperately. The French succeeded in pushing back the British, and they even managed to capture the orchard of La Haye Sainte and cut the farmhouse off from the rest of Wellington's forces. But these victories were short-lived, and the French were soon being repulsed.

Wellington placed troops on the reverse slope of Mont St. Jean, which helped to protect them from the French artillery. This was a favorite battle strategy of Wellington's, and likely helped spare him some casualties.

Around 4:00, the advance units of Blücher's Prussians were arriving on Napoléon's right flank, and Wellington was deploying them into the battle as quickly as possible. Napoléon realized that the Prussians were far from defeated. Grouchy had not succeeded in engaging them and keeping them pinned at Wavre.

Meanwhile, what of Grouchy? According to a story, he was at a farm eating strawberries with some of his commanders when the roar of Napoléon's artillery began, signaling the start of fighting.[6] Some of his commanders pleaded with him to turn around and head back to the sound of battle. Grouchy, however, overruled them. His orders were to chase the Prussians, and he was going to follow orders. Thus his 30,000 troops played no part in Waterloo, and Grouchy is often cited as the reason Napoléon lost.

By this time, around 4:00 or 4:30, with his battle strategy in tatters and the Prussians arriving in growing numbers on the battlefield, Napoléon knew that he should probably switch to a defensive strategy. But he had never gotten anywhere by being cautious and defensive. He decided to attack.

Artillery

Artillery in the Napoleonic Wars typically fired iron balls called roundshot, or "shot" for short. The strategy was to fire the shot about chest high from a flat surface. Since enemy soldiers were usually grouped tightly together, a single shot would rip through an enemy formation, tearing gory holes into people and causing many men to fall at once. Then, the cannonball would hit the hard ground and bounce along at high speed, inflicting more damage to soldiers as it went. Part of the effect of this weapon was psychological: a soldier who had just seen a shot tear through the men around him often either stopped in his tracks or simply turned around and headed for the rear. At Waterloo, because of the previous night's rain, the cannonballs tended to stick in the mud rather than bounce along.

Artillery was drawn by horses, since the guns and their carriages—the wooden supports on which they were mounted—could weigh thousands of pounds. If numerous horses in an artillery team were killed, the cannon could not be moved until the dead horses were cut out of their harnesses and dragged away, and living horses put in their place. Thus the loss of its horses could immobilize an artillery battery. Despite these drawbacks, artillery inflicted more than half the casualties Napoléon's enemies suffered in battle.[7]

Cuirass pierced by a cannonball at Waterloo

Chapter 5

The third phase of Waterloo began around 3:30 in the afternoon—before the second phase was over. The retreating French troops of d'Erlon reorganized and then attacked La Haye Sainte farmhouse in another attempt to break Wellington's center defenses.

In conjunction, the French launched a gigantic cavalry charge, also at the center of Wellington's defenses. Cavalry charges were another important part of Napoléon's military strategy. During his early years, the French cavalry was possibly the finest in Europe. Napoléon would turn it loose against an enemy's infantry that had already been weakened by artillery or infantry attacks. The sight of hundreds of horses thundering toward them with their riders shooting and waving swords was often too much for the beleaguered enemy troops. They typically broke ranks and ran.

However, that had been years before. Persistent warfare had worn down the French cavalry just as it had the rest of the army, and the cavalry that charged toward the British were no longer the finest in Europe. Although the force was between 9,000 and 10,000 soldiers, and

The Emperor Defeated

could have done considerable damage, the British were ready. They employed the one successful defensive strategy against cavalry charges: squares.

Strategists know that horses will not charge directly at soldiers who are pointing sharp objects at them, such as spears or bayonets. To repel cavalry charges, troops formed squares so that every soldier's back was protected by another. The horses, having nowhere to go, were forced to ride around the squares, leaving them vulnerable to heavy fire by the soldiers in the squares.

French cavalry led by Ney repeatedly smashed into the British squares from about 4:00 until 6:00. The fighting was described as "pandemonium" and "confused . . . chaotic."[1] One British soldier described it graphically: "During the battle

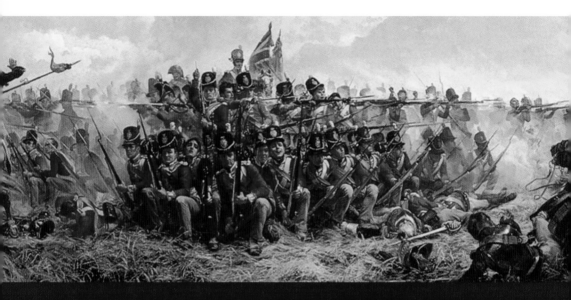

A battle strategy known as squares was an effective defense against charging cavalry. However, squares could be broken down by combining infantry and cavalry attacks, so the soldiers who formed the squares had to be vigilant against both types of threats.

our squares presented a shocking sight. Inside we were nearly suffocated by the smoke and smell from burnt cartridges. It was impossible to move a yard without treading upon a wounded comrade, or upon the bodies of the dead; and the loud groans of the wounded and dying were most appalling."[2]

The horses also suffered terribly in this maelstrom of death. One observer said the "ground was strewed with the fallen horses . . . we often saw a poor wounded animal raise its head, as if looking for its rider to afford him aid."[3]

The best way to combat squares was to combine cavalry charges with infantry attacks so that the infantry could disrupt the squares, but for some reason—debated to this day—Ney did not order the infantry to do this. The repeated cavalry charges were unsuccessful; not a single British square broke. By around 6:30 P.M., the cavalry charges ended. The fourth phase of the battle, and the one that brought Napoléon close to victory, was about to begin.

By this time, as Blücher's Prussians were streaming onto the battlefield, Napoléon won his greatest success when he forced the British to abandon La Haye Sainte. With only 42 of the original 400 defenders of La Haye Sainte left, the farmhouse roof on fire, and just a few rounds of ammunition for each man, the British were forced to retreat. Again the fighting was savage as the two sides battled over, around, and on top of the piles of bodies from previous assaults. The French were taking no prisoners; they bayoneted wounded enemy soldiers.

As the center of the British line wavered under the French assault, Napoléon had a golden opportunity to break the center of Wellington's line. One massive thrust likely would have sent the British hurtling backward. But the day's heavy fighting, combined with the increasing numbers of Prussians entering the fray, had drained Napoléon of reinforcements to throw into the breach in Wellington's line. He sorely felt the loss of Grouchy's men.

Ney, directing the assault on La Haye Sainte and realizing the opportunity he had to smash through the British defense, asked Napoléon for more troops. To this the emperor replied sarcastically: "Troops! Where do you want me to get them from? Do you want me to make them?"[4]

As Waterloo historian Jeremy Black points out, Napoléon did indeed have some reserves left—the Imperial Guard, his most trusted soldiers, the ones whom he always saved until later in a battle to clinch a victory and who had never let him down. Would Napoléon have gained a victory at Waterloo had he sent in his Imperial Guard at this critical moment? "History is an argument without end," wrote Dutch historian Pieter Geyl, and it will be forever debated as to what might have happened had Napoléon committed his Imperial Guard at this point.[5]

Meanwhile more and more Prussians were steadily arriving and pressuring Napoléon's right flank. With their numbers at 10,000 and growing, Napoléon may not have wanted to commit the Guard. As Black writes: "However successful Ney might be against the British, the French position risked dissolution if the Prussians maintained the pace of their advance."[6] Napoléon

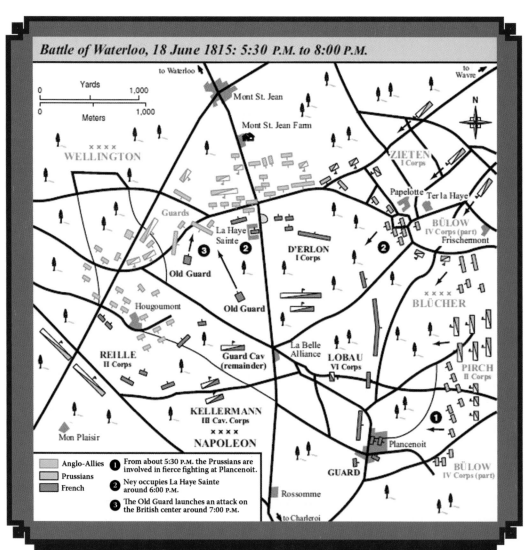

Battle of Waterloo, 18 June 1815: 5:30 P.M. to 8:00 P.M.

Yards

Meters

to Waterloo

to Wavre

Mont St. Jean

Mont St. Jean Farm

N

×××× WELLINGTON

ZIETEN
I Corps

Papelotte Ter la Haye

Guards

La Haye Sainte

BÜLOW
IV Corps (part)
Frischemont

D'ERLON
I Corps

Old Guard

BLÜCHER

Hougoumont

Old Guard

La Belle Alliance

REILLE
II Corps

Guard Cav
(remainder)

LOBAU
VI Corps

PIRCH
II Corps

KELLERMANN
III Cav. Corps

×××× NAPOLEON

Mon Plaisir

Plancenoit

Anglo-Allies	❶ From about 5:30 P.M. the Prussians are involved in fierce fighting at Plancenoit.
Prussians	❷ Ney occupies La Haye Sainte around 6:00 P.M.
French	❸ The Old Guard launches an attack on the British center around 7:00 P.M.

GUARD

BÜLOW
IV Corps (part)

Rossomme

to Charleroi

By the last two stages of the battle, the Prussians were arriving in greater and greater strength. Napoléon's forces, however, were depleted.

needed men to hold the Prussians off, so the Guard stayed put—for the time being.

At nearly 7:00 P.M., the sun was beginning to set on this exhausting and bloody day. Napoléon was running out of time. At last he decided to commit his Imperial Guard—approximately

When Napoléon sent in his Imperial Guard during the final phase of the battle, it represented his last chance for victory. It was also the climax of Napoléon's brilliant military career.

5,000 men—to the battle, hoping that they could continue their streak and secure another victory. This was the battle's fifth and final phase.

To boost his soldiers' confidence, Napoléon spread the word that Grouchy's troops had suddenly appeared on Wellington's left flank. This gave the French troops false hope; feeling that they were now part of turning the tide of battle instead of embarking on a desperate last-ditch charge, the Imperial Guard, dodging dead horses and humans, advanced on the British.

Wellington was prepared for this assault. Almost three dozen cannons filled with double grapeshot awaited the French, who were marching close together—perfect targets. When the cannons began firing, they tore huge holes into the neat French lines. Other British troops fired musketballs into the advancing French.

As the Imperial Guard approached, more than 1,000 British soldiers suddenly rose up from behind the crest of a ridge where Wellington had placed them. It is estimated that the Imperial Guard were no less than 40 yards away. At this point-blank range they were struck by a hurricane of musket balls. French soldiers dropped like dominoes. More than one-fifth of the group fell under the British guns.[7] The last great French charge of the Napoleonic Wars stopped dead.

After several minutes of bitter fighting, Wellington knew he could seal the victory. Rushing perilously close to the front, he ordered a bayonet charge. When the British soldiers saw him, some of them began cheering.

"No cheering, my lads, but forward and complete your victory!"[8] Wellington cried.

The French army fell apart under the allied onslaught and began a disorganized retreat, particularly when they realized that the troops that were advancing on them from the right were not Grouchy's men, but Prussians. The Prussian cavalry had also arrived, and they mercilessly cut down the retreating French.

Napoléon retreated south to Charleroi, tears streaming down his face.[9] The Battle of Waterloo, and the Napoleonic era, were over.

Aftermath

For a time after Waterloo, Napoléon wanted to keep fighting, unwilling—or unable—to concede that his cause was over. He was constantly figuring out where he could get more men—10,000 here, 15,000 there, and 30,000 from another place—and rebuild his shattered army. For several days what one writer called "the mad arithmetic" continued.[10]

On June 21 he returned to Paris, full of plans. The allied forces were marching to Paris, he told the delegates in the Chamber of Representatives. He must be given dictatorial powers to rally the country and throw the rascals out of France.

But the chamber had a different idea. Napoléon must go—and he did, abdicating on June 22. On July 15, 1815, he surrendered to the British ship HMS *Bellerophon*. He was taken to St. Helena, an isolated island far off the eastern coast of Africa, and removed from civilization. He died there on May 5, 1821.

French casualties at Waterloo were 25,000 killed and wounded. British casualties were 15,000, and the Prussians lost 7,000. For days the corpses of men and horses littered the battlefield, bloated in the June heat. Reportedly the smell was so nauseating that the horses pulling the wagons that picked up the bodies screamed in distress.

After the battle Wellington rode in silence to his headquarters, with the sound of wounded men and horses ringing in his ears. There he dined alone. Each time the door opened, he looked up anxiously, hoping to see one of the many young aides or officers who had eaten breakfast with him that day. Each time he was disappointed. Finally, when all hope of seeing anybody was gone, and with one of his favorite aides lying wounded and dying in his bed, Wellington lay down on a pallet and went to sleep.[11]

All dates 1815

March 1	Napoléon returns to France from Elba; he reaches Paris on March 20. The Seventh Coalition forms.
June 12	Napoléon leaves Paris, intending to attack the British and Prussian armies separately before other members of the coalition can join them.
June 15	Napoléon crosses into modern-day Belgium.
June 16	At the Battle of Ligny, Napoléon defeats the Prussians. The Battle of Quatre Bras features the British Army against other French forces.
June 18	(all times approximate)
11:30 A.M.	The Battle of Waterloo begins. The French attack the Hougoumont farmhouse complex.
1:30 P.M.	French infantry assault is launched against the center of the English defense.
3:30	D'Erlon attacks La Haye Sainte farmhouse. The French launch a massive cavalry assault against the English. The British form into squares for defense.
6:30	The French finally capture La Haye Sainte farmhouse complex.
7:00	The French Imperial Guard launches a final assault. It fails. The French retreat.
June 21	Napoléon returns to Paris, asking for dictatorial powers.
June 22	Napoléon abdicates.
July 15	Napoléon leaves for exile on St. Helena.

History and Technology Timeline

1756	The Seven Years' War between Prussia and Austria begins; it eventually involves all of Europe and the North American territories before it ends in 1763.
1763	Surveying begins for the Mason-Dixon Line between Maryland and Pennsylvania.
1765	Britain passes the Stamp Act in its North American colonies.
1769	Napoléon Bonaparte is born.

1773	Protesters against British taxes on the American colonies stage the Boston Tea Party.
1775	The battles of Lexington and Concord in Massachusetts mark the beginning of the Revolutionary War.
1776	Thomas Jefferson writes the Declaration of Independence.
1778	France joins the American Revolution against Great Britain.
1781	Lord Cornwallis surrenders to George Washington at Yorktown, effectively ending the Revolutionary War.
1788	The U.S. Constitution is ratified.
1792	After the successful French Revolution, the monarchy is overthrown and the First Republic begins.
1801	Great Britain and Ireland merge to form the United Kingdom.
1803	In the Louisiana Purchase, Napoléon sells Louisiana, France's claim in North America, to the United States for $15 million.
1812	The War of 1812 between the U.S. and Great Britain begins. In June, Napoléon invades Russia.
1814	Napoléon abdicates as emperor of France and is exiled to Elba. Louis XVIII becomes king of France.
1815	Napoléon rebuilds his army and fights at Waterloo.
1820	In the Missouri Compromise, Maine is admitted to the Union as a free state and Missouri is admitted as a slave state.
1821	Napoléon dies on May 5.
1836	The Arc de Triomphe, commissioned by Napoléon in 1806, is finished in Paris. This monument commemorates Napoléon's Grand Armée.
1846	The United States goes to war with Mexico over territory in the southwest. Thousands of people flee Ireland when the potato famine causes mass starvation there.
1848	The last king to rule France, Louis-Philippe, is ousted, and Charles-Louis-Napoléon Bonaparte becomes president of France.
1854	The Kansas-Nebraska Act repeals the Missouri Compromise.
1861	The American Civil War begins.

Chapter 1. The Fight for Hougoumont

1. Frank McLynn, *Napoléon* (New York: Arcade Publishing, 2002), p. 613.
2. Ibid.
3. Jeremy Black, *The Battle of Waterloo* (New York: Random House, 2010), p. 99.
4. Jac Weller, *Wellington at Waterloo* (New York: Thomas Y. Crowell Company, 1967), p. 90.

Chapter 2. Captain Cannon

1. Vincent Cronin, *Napoléon Bonaparte* (New York: William Morrow & Company, Inc., 1972), p. 20.
2. Fairfax Downey, *Cannonade* (Garden City, New York: Doubleday & Company, Inc., 1966), p. 157.
3. Ibid., p. 156.
4. John Norris, *Artillery* (Gloucestershire, UK: Sutton Publishing Limited, 2000), p. 130.
5. Ibid., p. 132.
6. Downey, p. 166.
7. Colonel Trevor N. Dupuy, *The Evolution of Weapons and Warfare* (Indianapolis, Indiana: The Bobbs-Merrill Company, Inc., 1980), p. 158.
8. Cronin, p. 258.
9. Norris, p. 131.

Chapter 3. Why Waterloo?

1. Andrew Roberts, *Waterloo* (New York: Harper Collins, 2005), p. 9.
2. Ibid., p. 22.
3. Ibid., p. 24.
4. Elizabeth Longford, *Wellington: The Years of the Sword* (New York: Harper & Row, 1969), p. 421.
5. André Castelot, *Napoléon* (New York: Harper & Row, 1967), p. 543.
6. Roberts, p. 36.
7. Jeremy Black, *The Battle of Waterloo* (New York: Random House, 2010), p. 89.

Chapter 4. The Battle Begins

1. Andrew Roberts, *Waterloo* (New York: Harper Collins, 2005), p. 40.
2. Vincent Cronin, *Napoléon Bonaparte* (New York: William Morrow & Company, Inc., 1972), p. 400.
3. Jeremy Black, *The Battle of Waterloo* (New York: Random House, 2010), p. 97.
4. Roberts, p. 57.
5. Black, p. 95.
6. Ibid., p. 72.
7. Colonel Trevor N. Dupuy, *The Evolution of Weapons and Warfare* (Indianapolis, Indiana: The Bobbs-Merrill Company, Inc., 1980), p. 158.

Chapter 5. The Emperor Defeated

1. Andrew Roberts, *Waterloo* (New York: Harper Collins, 2005), p. 82.
2. Ibid., p. 84.
3. Ibid.
4. Ibid., p. 94.
5. Ibid., p. 95.
6. Jeremy Black, *The Battle of Waterloo* (New York: Random House, 2010), p. 133.
7. Ibid., p. 143.
8. Elizabeth Longford, *Wellington: The Years of the Sword* (New York: Harper & Row, 1969), p. 478.
9. Stephan Coote, *Napoléon and the Hundred Days* (Cambridge, Massachusetts: Da Capo Press, 2004), p. 247.
10. Ibid., p. 249.
11. Elizabeth Longford, *Wellington: The Years of the Sword* (New York: Harper & Row, 1969), p. 484.

Further Reading

Books

Greenblatt, Miriam. *Napoléon Bonaparte and Imperial France.* New York: Benchmark Books, 2005.

Nardo, Don. *France.* New York: Children's Press, 2008.

Schlaepfer, Gloria G. *The Louisiana Purchase.* New York: Franklin Watts, 2005.

Tidmarsh, Celia. *France.* Mankato, Minnesota: Sea to Sea Publications, 2009.

PHOTO CREDITS: Cover picture—Robert Alexander Hillingford; pp. 1, 36—Elizabeth Thompson; pp. 4–5—Clémente-Auguste Andrieux; p. 7—Keith Rocco; pp. 9, 12, 13, 15, 18–19, 22, 23, 26–27, 28, 29, 33, 34–35, 38, 47—cc-by-sa; pp. 10–11, 14, 32—Charles Horace Vernet; p. 16—Peter Isotalo; pp. 8, 21, 31—Barbara Marvis; p. 24—Johann Emil Hünten; p. 30—George Jones; p. 39—Harry Payne. Every effort has been made to locate all copyright holders of materials used in this book. Any errors or omissions will be corrected in future editions of the book.

Works Consulted

Black, Jeremy. *The Battle of Waterloo.* New York: Random House, 2010.

Castelot, André. *Napoléon.* New York: Harper & Row, 1967.

Coote, Stephan. *Napoléon and the Hundred Days.* Cambridge, Massachusetts: Da Capo Press, 2004.

Cronin, Vincent. *Napoléon Bonaparte.* New York: William Morrow & Company, Inc., 1972.

Downey, Fairfax. *Cannonade.* Garden City, New York: Doubleday & Company, Inc., 1966.

Dupuy, Colonel Trevor N. *The Evolution of Weapons and Warfare.* Indianapolis, Indiana: The Bobbs-Merrill Company, Inc., 1980.

Korngold, Ralph. *The Last Years of Napoléon.* New York: Harcourt, Brace and Company, 1959.

Longford, Elizabeth. *Wellington: The Years of the Sword.* New York: Harper & Row, 1969.

McLynn, Frank. *Napoléon.* New York: Arcade Publishing, 2002.

Norris, John. *Artillery.* Gloucestershire: Sutton Publishing Limited, 2000.

Roberts, Andrew. *Napoléon and Wellington.* New York: Simon & Schuster, 2001.

———. *Waterloo.* New York: HarperCollins, 2005.

Thompson, J. M. *Napoléon Bonaparte.* New York: Oxford University Press, 1952.

Weller, Jac. *Wellington at Waterloo.* New York: Thomas Y. Crowell Company, 1967.

On the Internet

BBC British History in Depth—The Battle of Waterloo
http://www.bbc.co.uk/history/british/empire_seapower/battle_waterloo_01.shtml

British Battles.com: The Battle of Waterloo
http://www.britishbattles.com/waterloo/waterloo-june-1815.htm

Eyewitness to History: The Battle of Waterloo, 1815
http://www.eyewitnesstohistory.com/waterloo.htm

Waterloo Battlefield, Lion Hamlet, Belgium
http://www.waterloo1815.be/en/waterloo/

abdicate (AB-dih-kayt)—To give up a position of power, such as a throne, in a formal manner.

conscription (kun-SKRIP-shun)—The practice of requiring people to enroll in military service.

cuirass (kwih-RASS)—A piece of armor that covers the body from the neck to the waist.

debilitate (dee-BIH-lih-tayt)—To make weak or feeble.

deploy (dee-PLOY)—To arrange and place troops into position.

dissolution (dis-oh-LOO-shun)—The falling apart, breaking up, or dissolving of something.

exile (EK-syl)—The forced removal from one's native land.

hallucination (huh-loo-sih-NAY-shun)—The experience of thinking you see, feel, or hear something that is not there.

ordnance (ORD-nints)—Military weapons and the ammunition and equipment that go with them.

partisan (PAR-tih-sin)—Someone who supports a leader or cause.

relentless (ree-LENT-liss)—Not stopping.

sanguine (SAN-gwin)—Hopeful or confident; relaxed.

strategist (STRAT-eh-jist)—Someone who works out a plan (strategy) and carries it out.

terrain (ter-AYN)—The shape and features of a piece of land.

thwart (THWORT)—To disrupt the success of a plan.

Arc de Triomphe de l'Étoile, a memorial to those who fought and died for France in the French Revolution and the Napoleonic Wars

Index

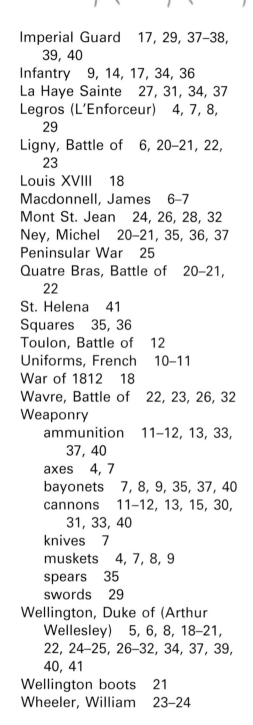